Aircraft

Michael J. H. Taylor

Illustrated by
Michael Roffe

Piccolo
A Piper Book

Contents

Edited by Angela Royston

Introduction

The modern aircraft is fast, safe and comfortable to travel in. It has changed a lot since the first aeroplanes flew about eighty years ago. It is hard to imagine a simpler-looking shape for an airliner than today's Concorde, similar in many ways to a dart-plane you can fold from a sheet of paper. Yet Concorde can fly as fast as a Royal Air Force fighter and reach America without stopping to refuel. This shows how interesting it is to know more about the aircraft you see at airports. Only if you can identify an aircraft can you tell how modern it is, how fast it can fly and how many passengers it can carry.

There are more than 200 airports, airfields and Air Force bases in England, Scotland, Wales and Northern Ireland. The most important are London's Heathrow and Gatwick airports. In 1983, well over 283,000 flights in or out of Heathrow were made, making it the busiest international airport in the world. More than 27 million passengers used Heathrow that year, 101,935 on one day alone. There are many regional airports in the UK, one probably quite near to where you live.

Helicopters fly from airports, but there are several special heliports, the most important being at Battersea and Penzance. Some hotels and companies have their own heliports for important people. Many different light planes can be seen at the large number of flying clubs throughout the UK.

Often there is more than one version of the same aeroplane. This is because a manufacturer may improve the aeroplane during production, or alter slightly its size or seating arrangements. Series or Mark means version.

Before going to an airport to spot aircraft, read this book carefully. And remember, not all aeroplanes and helicopters you will see are described in this book. How many other types can you spot?

What to Look For

When you begin to identify an aircraft, count the number of engines it has. If it has three or four turn to pages 14 to 21 and try to identify it from the pictures. Look at where the engines are, the shape of the fuselage, wings and tail. Aeroplanes with two engines are on pages 22 to 27. Planes with propellers are on pages 28 to 37. Helicopters and small aeroplanes follow from page 38. Use the insignia drawings on pages 8 to 13 to tell which airline flies the aeroplane and from what country. Fill in the spotter's record box the first time you see each kind of aircraft.

When you are familiar with the shape of aircraft, you will be able to recognize them in the air. The silhouettes given show the shape of each aeroplane in flight. They are not drawn to scale, and so do not show the size of one with another.

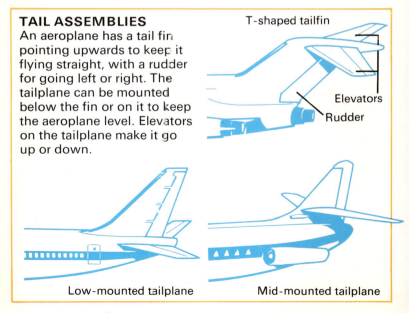

TAIL ASSEMBLIES
An aeroplane has a tail fin pointing upwards to keep it flying straight, with a rudder for going left or right. The tailplane can be mounted below the fin or on it to keep the aeroplane level. Elevators on the tailplane make it go up or down.

T-shaped tailfin

Elevators

Rudder

Low-mounted tailplane

Mid-mounted tailplane

ENGINE ARRANGEMENTS

Most modern airliners are powered by turbofan engines. Concorde is an exception and uses four turbojets. The most common arrangements are for the engines to be mounted under the wings, or two under the wings and one in the tail. But several airliners you are likely to see have all rear-mounted engines. These include the Trident. Only very old or smaller aircraft with propellers have piston engines, the rest use turboprops.

Airbus A300B One large turbofan under each wing.

DC-9 One small turbofan each side of the rear fuselage.

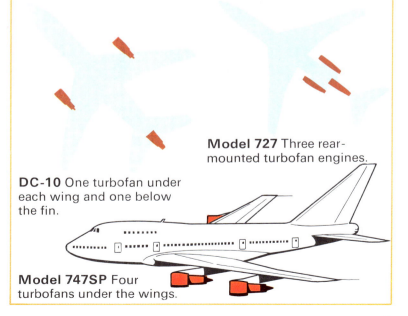

Model 727 Three rear-mounted turbofan engines.

DC-10 One turbofan under each wing and one below the fin.

Model 747SP Four turbofans under the wings.

KINDS OF ENGINE

Piston engines are used on most small aircraft and modern light transports up to Islander size. The engine drives a propeller.

A turbofan (above) is like a turbojet with normally a huge fan at the front to suck in great amounts of air. Most air goes past the combustion chamber to mix with the exhaust to give more power.

A turboprop (below) is like a turbofan but with a propeller at the front instead of a covered fan. It burns less fuel than a turbojet and is used on slower transports.

Turbojet engines (above) are noisier and burn more fuel than turbofans, but are generally smaller.

INSIDE AN AIRLINER

An airliner takes many years and millions of pounds to design and build. The manufacturer must be sure that it is safe, comfortable and reliable, as well as economic to run. The number, type and arrangement of engines affect its performance and success. Engine makers compete for the order to supply the engines. With modern airliners, the number of seats can be altered to suit the number of passengers that will regularly fly.
In the case of this TriStar, work began in 1966 to find out the type of aircraft needed by customers. The first aircraft flew on 16 November 1970 and services began in 1972.

Tailfin

Rudder

Air duct to engine

Rolls-Royce RB 211 engine

Elevators

Tailplane

GLOSSARY

Combustion chamber Part of the engine where fuel and air are burned.

Delta wings Wings that look triangular from above or below.

Fuselage The main body of an aircraft.

Helipad Prepared ground for use by helicopters.

Heliport Special airport for helicopters only.

Insignia Painted symbol of an airline or company.

Long-range Further than medium-range.

Medium-range Up to 6500 kilometres while carrying maximum payload.

Prototype First one built for flight testing.

Series Version (for example, BAe One-Eleven Series 400).

Short-range Under 2225 kilometres.

Supersonic Faster than the speed of sound.

VIP Very important person.

Wide-body Wide fuselage for three columns of seats.

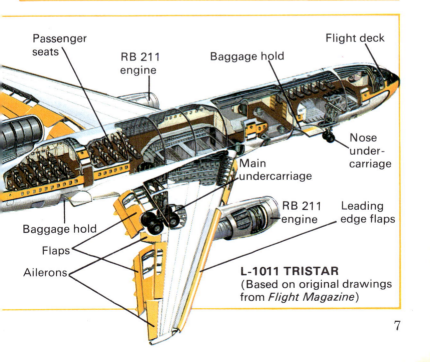

Passenger seats — RB 211 engine — Baggage hold — Flight deck — Nose under-carriage — Main undercarriage — RB 211 engine — Leading edge flaps — Baggage hold — Flaps — Ailerons

L-1011 TRISTAR
(Based on original drawings from *Flight Magazine*)

Airline Insignia

Each aeroplane or helicopter you see that is flown by an airline company will have a painted symbol. This can usually be seen on the tail. Look at it carefully and match it with the illustrations on the next five pages. This will tell you the name of the airline and what country it comes from. Sometimes the name of the airline or the country it comes from is written on the fuselage in big letters. But remember, not all insignias you may see are drawn in this book.

Each country has special registration letters. Every aircraft from that country has to show these letters on the fuselage. British aircraft have the letter G. A typical British registration is G-BGJE. Each insignia drawn here has its country registration by it. Some airlines only fly to the UK on charter.

Aer Lingus (Republic of Ireland EI)

Aeroflot (Soviet Union CCCP)

Air Algérie (Algeria 7T)

Air Canada (Canada C)

Air Europe (United Kingdom G)

Air France (France F)

Air-India
(India VT)

Air Malta
(Malta 9H)

Air UK
(United Kingdom G)

Alia
(Jordan JY)

Alitalia
(Italy I)

Austrian Airlines
(Austria OE)

Balkan Bulgarian
Airlines (Bulgaria LZ)

Braathens-SAFE
(Norway LN)

Britannia Airways
(United Kingdom G)

British Airways
(United Kingdom G)

British Caledonian
(United Kingdom G)

BWIA International
(Trinidad & Tobago 9Y)

Cathay Pacific
(Hong Kong VR-H)

CP Air
(Canada C)

CSA
(Czechoslovakia OK)

Cyprus Airways
(Cyprus 5B)

Dan-Air
(United Kingdom G)

Egyptair
(Egypt SU)

El Al
(Israel 4X)

Ethiopian Airlines
(Ethiopia ET)

Finnair
(Finland OH)

Gulf Air
(Oman A40)

Iberia
(Spain EC)

Interflug
(East Germany DDR)

Iraqi Airways
(Iraq YI)

Iran Air
(Iran EP)

Japan Air Lines
(Japan JA)

JAT
(Yugoslavia YU)

Kenya Airways
(Kenya 5Y)

KLM
(Netherlands PH)

Kuwait Airways
(Kuwait 9K)

Libyan Arab Airlines
(Libya 5A)

LOT
(Poland SP)

Lufthansa
(West Germany D)

Malev
(Hungary HA)

MEA
(Lebanon OD)

Northwest Orient
(United States N)

Olympic Airways
(Greece SX)

Pakistan International
(Pakistan AP)

Pan Am
(United States N)

Qantas
(Australia VH)

Royal Air Maroc
(Morocco CN)

Sabena
(Belgium OO)

SAS (Denmark OY,
Norway LN, Sweden SE)

Saudia
(Saudi Arabia HZ)

Singapore Airlines
(Singapore 9V)

South African Airways
(South Africa ZS)

Sterling Airways
(Denmark OY)

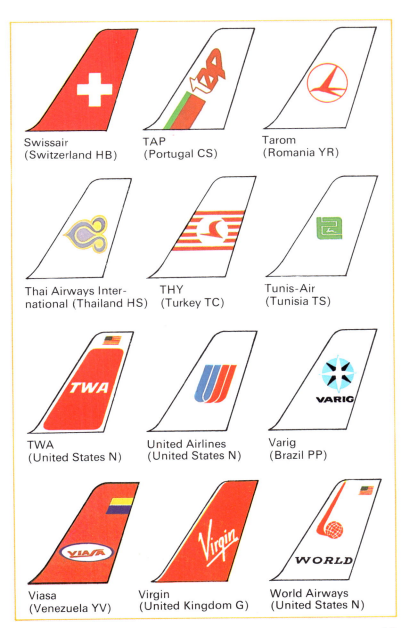

Swissair
(Switzerland HB)

TAP
(Portugal CS)

Tarom
(Romania YR)

Thai Airways Inter-
national (Thailand HS)

THY
(Turkey TC)

Tunis-Air
(Tunisia TS)

TWA
(United States N)

United Airlines
(United States N)

Varig
(Brazil PP)

Viasa
(Venezuela YV)

Virgin
(United Kingdom G)

World Airways
(United States N)

Three and Four-Engined Airliners

The first passenger services were started in 1910 in Germany using airships. After World War I bombers were made into airliners, and international passenger flights began in 1919 between Paris and London.

Soon it was realized that aircraft with more than one engine were safer, as they could carry on if an engine failed.

Today all the world's long-range airliners have three or four engines. They have to carry a heavy fuel load to avoid wasting time on refuelling stops. They have also to carry enough passengers to pay for the flight. The fewer the engines the bigger they have to be to give the power. The largest commercial passenger airliner in use today is the Boeing 747, and the fastest is Concorde, both of which have four engines.

BAe/AÉROSPATIALE CONCORDE

Concorde is the only airliner in service today which can fly supersonically. It can cruise at 2179 km/h, more than twice the speed of sound. Passenger services began on 21 January 1976. British Airways operates

BAe 146

The 146 is the newest British jet airliner. It first flew in 1981. Though most have been exported, Dan-Air is a UK operator.

146 Series 100

Wing span: 26·34 m
Length: 26.16 m
Cruising speed: 778 km/h
Passengers: 71 to 93
Engines: Four turbofans

DATE _____

PLACE _____

INSIGNIA _____

Concordes to the United States from London's Heathrow. Concorde can be recognized easily by its huge delta wings and pointed nose. The nose droops on take-off and landing to give the pilots a better forward view.

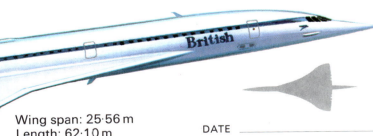

Wing span: 25·56 m
Length: 62·10 m
Cruising speed: 2179 km/h
Passengers: Normally 100
Engines: Four turbojets

DATE _____

PLACE _____

INSIGNIA _____

BOEING 707

The oldest jet airliner in use, the 707 entered service in 1958. It was a giant airliner for its time. Many are still flown as medium/long-range airliners, but the 707 is no longer built.

707-320C
Wing span: 44·42 m
Length: 46·61 m
Cruising speed: 973 km/h
Passengers: Up to 219
Engines: Four turbofans

DATE _____

PLACE _____

INSIGNIA _____

BOEING 727

Advanced 727-200
Wing span: 32·92 m
Length: 46·69 m
Cruising speed: 964 km/h
Passengers: Up to 189
Engines: Three turbofans

The 727 is a short/medium-range airliner. It first flew in 1963. It is the only Boeing airliner with rear-mounted engines. Over 1800 have been sold, more than any other type. The 131-passenger 727-100 was followed by the longer -200.

DATE _____

PLACE _____

INSIGNIA _____

BOEING 747 AND 747SP

The 747, the Jumbo Jet, was the first airliner with a very wide body, and it can seat 516 passengers in rows of ten. When it carries fewer passengers the upper deck cabin can be used as a lounge by first-class passengers. It is a heavy long-range airliner. More than 600 have been sold. It began passenger services in 1970 and today nearly 5 million people fly in 747s each month. A version of the 747 with a shorter fuselage and a lower weight is the 747SP. SP means special performance as it can carry 321–440 people longer distances.

747
Wing span: 59·64 m
Length: 70·66 m
Maximum speed: 969 km/h
Passengers: 452 to 516
Engines: Four turbofans

DATE _____

PLACE_____

INSIGNIA _____

DATE _____

PLACE_____

INSIGNIA _____

747SP

HAWKER SIDDELEY TRIDENT

The Trident is a
short/medium-range airliner.
First flown in 1962, the
original 103-seater Trident 1
was followed by bigger and
longer-range versions. The
180-seater Trident 3B first
flew in 1969.

Trident 2E
Wing span: 29·87 m
Length: 34·97 m
Cruising speed: 972 km/h
Passengers: Up to 132
Engines: Three turbofans

DATE _____

PLACE _____

INSIGNIA _____

ILYUSHIN Il-62

The Il-62 is a Soviet long-
range airliner. It first flew in
1963. About 200 were built.
The Soviet airline Aeroflot
put the Il-62 into service in
1967. The latest version is
the more powerful Il-62MK.

Il-62MK
Wing span: 43·20 m
Length: 53·12 m
Cruising speed: 900 km/h
Passengers: Up to 195
Engines: Four rear turbofans

DATE _____

PLACE _____

INSIGNIA _____

ILYUSHIN Il-86

This was the first Soviet wide-body airliner. It first flew in 1977 and entered service with Aeroflot in 1980. A longer-range version could be the Il-96.

Wing span: 48·06 m
Length: 59·54 m
Cruising speed: 950 km/h
Passengers: Up to 350
Engines: Four turbofans

DATE _____

PLACE _____

INSIGNIA _____

LOCKHEED L-1011 TRISTAR

The TriStar is a medium/long-range airliner and can carry many passengers thanks to its wide-body fuselage. It first flew in 1970. More than 240 have been sold, many to British Airways.
Wing span: 47·34 m
Length: 54·17 m

Cruising speed: 964 km/h
Passengers: 256 to 400
Engines: Three turbofans

DATE _____

PLACE _____

INSIGNIA _____

McDONNELL DOUGLAS DC-8 SERIES

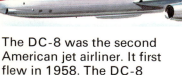

The DC-8 was the second American jet airliner. It first flew in 1958. The DC-8 Series 50, the last version of the early DC-8 models, is still in regular use.
Wing span: 43·41 m
Length: 45·87 m
Cruising speed: 933 km/h
Passengers: Up to 179
Engines: Four turbojets or turbofans

DATE _____

PLACE _____

INSIGNIA _____

McDONNELL DOUGLAS DC-8 SUPER SIXTY and SUPER SEVENTY SERIES

In 1965 the fuselage of a DC-8 Series 50 was lengthened. The new plane was called the DC-8 Super Sixty, and many were built in several versions for long and very long-range flights. Later, some were fitted with more powerful engines, to become Super Seventies.

Super 71
Wing span: 45·23 m
Length: 57·12 m
Maximum speed: 965 km/h
Passengers: 189 or 259
Engines: Four turbofans

DATE _____

PLACE _____

INSIGNIA _____

20

McDONNELL DOUGLAS DC-10

The DC-10 and TriStar are similar to look at. The DC-10's third engine is, however, mounted under the tailfin. It is a medium/long-range wide-body airliner. It first flew in 1970. More than 360 have been ordered.
Wing span: 50·41 m
Length: 55·50 m

Cruising speed: 908 km/h
Passengers: 255 to 380
Engines: Three turbofans

DATE _____

PLACE _____

INSIGNIA _____

TUPOLEV Tu-154

Looking like a scaled-up Boeing 727, the Soviet Tu-154 is a medium/long-range airliner. It first flew in 1968. About 350 have been built in several versions. It is now flown to the UK by Aeroflot, Balkan Bulgarian Airlines, Malev and Tarom.
Wing span: 37·55 m
Length: 47·90 m

Cruising speed: 900 km/h
Passengers: 128 to 168
Engines: Three turbofans

DATE _____

PLACE _____

INSIGNIA _____

Twin-Engined Airliners

Some of the oldest and newest airliners in service today have two engines. At one end of the time scale is the Caravelle, which first flew in 1955, and at the other end are the latest Boeings, the 757 and the 767. All the airliners in this section have short or medium ranges and are generally smaller, lighter and slower than airliners with more engines. They are normally used for domestic or shorter international flights.

New twin-engined airliners are now under development. These include the European Airbus A320, which will have a narrow-body type of fuselage seating up to 179 passengers. No prototype has yet flown. The Soviet Tupolev Tu-204, the expected future replacement for the Tu-154 type, may also be a twin-engined airliner.

AIRBUS A300 and A310

The A300 is a short/medium-range, wide-body airliner. It is a truly European effort, with companies from France, Germany, the UK, the Netherlands and Spain taking part in its design and construction. It first entered service in May 1974 with Air France, flying between Paris and London. Passenger and freighter versions are built. All are quiet and economic to operate. Well over 200 are in use.

The A310 was developed from the A300. It has a shorter fuselage for 210 to

234 passengers normally (280 maximum), and new wings of a more advanced design. It can fly further than the A300.

AÉROSPATIALE SE 210 CARAVELLE

The French Caravelle was the first jet airliner to have its engines mounted on the rear of the fuselage. It entered service in May 1959 and 280 were built.

Caravelle 12
Wing span: 34·30 m
Length: 36·24 m
Cruising speed: 825 km/h
Passengers: Up to 139
Engines: Two turbofans

DATE _____

PLACE _____

INSIGNIA _____

A300
Wing span: 44·84 m
Length: 53·62 m
Cruising speed: 911 km/h
Passengers: 220 to 336
Engines: Two large turbofans

DATE _____

PLACE _____

INSIGNIA _____

BAe ONE-ELEVEN

The One-Eleven is a short-range airliner with a turbofan engine on each side of the rear fuselage. Viewed from the side it is similar to the DC-9. However, its tailfin is not so rounded. The Series 200 entered service in 1965. Altogether, 143 Series 200/300/400/475s were built. The longer Series 500 (bottom) seats up to 119 passengers instead of the usual 89. It has a slightly greater wing span and more powerful engines. It was first delivered in 1968 and many are in service. Today the One-Eleven is only built in Romania.

DATE _____

PLACE _____

INSIGNIA _____

Series 500
Wing span: 28·50 m
Length: 32·61 m
Cruising speed: 870 km/h
Passengers: 97 to 119
Engines: Two turbofans

DATE _____

PLACE _____

INSIGNIA _____

BOEING 737

Wing span: 28·35 m
Length: 30·53 m
Cruising speed: 856 km/h
Passengers: Up to 149
Engines: Two turbofans

The 737 is the baby of all Boeing airliners. It is a short-range plane with two turbofans under the wings. It entered service in 1968. Well over 1100 have been sold.

DATE _____

PLACE _____

INSIGNIA _____

BOEING 757

The 757 is the newest Boeing airliner to fly, first taking off in 1982. It is a short/medium-range aircraft. British Airways was one of the first airlines to put it into use, in early 1983.

Wing span: 37·95 m
Length: 47·32 m
Cruising speed: 898 km/h
Passengers: Up to 239
Engines: Two turbofans

DATE _____

PLACE _____

INSIGNIA _____

BOEING 767

Boeing's newest wide-body airliner is the 767. It is a medium-range aircraft that first flew in 1981. The UK's Britannia Airways used two in 1984, with two more arriving in 1985.

Wing span: 47·57 m
Length: 48·51 m
Cruising speed: 898 km/h
Passengers: 211 to 289
Engines: Two turbofans

DATE _____

PLACE _____

INSIGNIA _____

TUPOLEV Tu-134

The Tu-134 is the Soviet equal to the One-Eleven or DC-9. It was designed as an improved version of the older Tu-124. It has rear-mounted engines and a T-shape tail. International passenger services with the Tu-134 began in 1967. The original 64 to 72-passenger Tu-134 was followed by the Tu-134A. This version is slightly longer to carry more passengers. About 300 Tu-134/134As were built. Aeroflot flies the largest number to the UK. Some Tu-

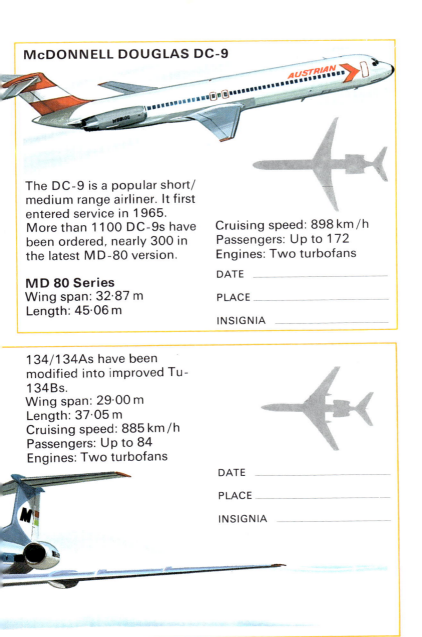

McDONNELL DOUGLAS DC-9

The DC-9 is a popular short/medium range airliner. It first entered service in 1965. More than 1100 DC-9s have been ordered, nearly 300 in the latest MD-80 version.

MD 80 Series
Wing span: 32·87 m
Length: 45·06 m

Cruising speed: 898 km/h
Passengers: Up to 172
Engines: Two turbofans

DATE _____

PLACE _____

INSIGNIA _____

134/134As have been modified into improved Tu-134Bs.
Wing span: 29·00 m
Length: 37·05 m
Cruising speed: 885 km/h
Passengers: Up to 84
Engines: Two turbofans

DATE _____

PLACE _____

INSIGNIA _____

27

Propeller-Driven Airliners

This section of the book has the greatest variety of aircraft. Some, like the Twin Otter, are small when compared to the mighty Hercules or Belfast. Engines also vary a lot. Aircraft with two small piston engines are included alongside others with four big turboprops.

Some of the oldest aircraft included in this section are used today as freighters. These provide important transport services, and can be chartered to carry heavy or bulky freight or animals. Another old plane is the Viscount, the world's first airliner with turboprop engines. But modern types are included – like the Shorts 330 and 360. They are used for commuter and regional services, flying people from such out-of-the way places as the Scottish islands to major centres.

ARMSTRONG WHITWORTH ARGOSY

The Argosy will be one of the most difficult aircraft to spot. It is a freighter with two booms between the wings and tail. It was first flown in 1959. The illustration shows an Air Bridge Carriers' Argosy 101.

Wing span: 33·05 m
Length: 26·44 m
Cruising speed: 451 km/h
Freight: Up to 12,000 kg
Engines: Four turboprops

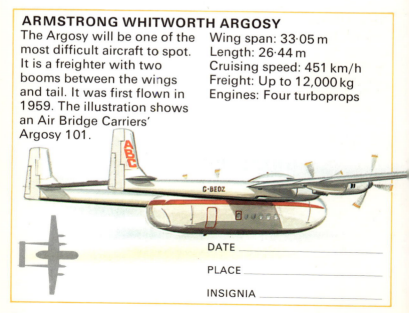

DATE _____

PLACE _____

INSIGNIA _____

BAe HS 748

The 748 is a short/medium-range passenger or cargo transport that has operated since 1962. Many have been sold, but mostly for export. Two are used by the Queen's Flight of the RAF to carry the Royal Family.

Wing span: 31·23 m
Length: 20·42 m
Cruising speed: 452 km/h
Passengers: 40 to 58
Engines: Two turboprops

DATE _____

PLACE _____

INSIGNIA _____

BEECHCRAFT 99 and CESSNA TITAN

These similar planes are used as passenger, executive and light cargo transports. The 99 has been used since 1968. In 1976 10-seater piston-engined Titans began flying. Several British air-taxi companies fly Titans.

99
Wing span: 13·98 m
Length: 13·58 m

Cruising speed: 460 km/h
Passengers: 15
Engines: Two turboprops

DATE _____

PLACE _____

INSIGNIA _____

CANADAIR CL-44

Only a very small number of CL-44s fly to the UK. It was built in Canada as a freighter version of the Britannia. The CL-44D4 version has a 'swing tail' – the tail of the fuselage is hinged to open like a door to make loading easier.
Wing span: 43·37 m
Length: 46·28 m
Cruising speed: 612 km/h
Engines: Four turboprops

DATE _____

PLACE _____

INSIGNIA _____

DE HAVILLAND DHC-6 TWIN OTTER

The Twin Otter is a very successful general purpose light transport aircraft. It can take-off and land in very short distances. More than 800 have been sold since 1966. Several are flown in the UK.
Wing span: 19 81 m
Length: 15·77 m

Cruising speed: 338 km/h
Passengers: Up to 20
Engines: Two turboprops

DATE _____

PLACE _____

INSIGNIA _____

DE HAVILLAND DHC-7 DASH 7

The Dash 7 is a short/medium-range transport plane. Like the Twin Otter it can take-off and land in short distances. It is also quiet to operate. It entered service in America in 1978. Brymon and Loganair in the UK received Dash 7s.
Wing span: 28·35 m
Length: 24·58 m

Cruising speed: 428 km/h
Passengers: Up to 50
Engines: Four turboprops

DATE _____

PLACE _____

INSIGNIA _____

EMBRAER EMB-110 BANDEIRANTE

The Bandeirante is a small transport aircraft. It is built in Brazil. It first flew in 1972. Many versions are built with 7, 12, 15 or more seats or cargo space. Over 400 have been delivered to customers.
Wing span: 15·33 m
Length: 15·10 m
Cruising speed: 413 km/h
Passengers: 15 to 21
Engines: Two turboprops

DATE _____

PLACE _____

INSIGNIA _____

31

FOKKER F.27 FRIENDSHIP

The Friendship is a popular smallish medium-range airliner. It is built in the Netherlands. Passenger services in America and by Aer Lingus in Ireland began in 1958. Many hundreds of Friendships have been sold.
Wing span: 29·00 m
Length: 23·56 m
Cruising speed: 480 km/h
Passengers: 44 to 60
Engines: Two turboprops

DATE _____

PLACE _____

INSIGNIA _____

HANDLEY PAGE HERALD

The Herald is a short-range airliner. It was designed to have four piston engines but this was later changed to two turboprops. It entered service in 1960. Quite a few are flown in the UK.
Wing span: 28·88 m
Length: 23·01 m
Cruising speed: 433 km/h
Passengers: Up to 56
Engines: Two turboprops

DATE _____

PLACE _____

INSIGNIA _____

ILYUSHIN Il-18

This Soviet medium-range airliner is even older than the similar British Vanguard/ Merchantman. It entered service in 1959. About 800 were built. The Polish airline LOT flies passenger and cargo versions into the UK.
Wing span: 37·40 m
Length: 35·90 m

Cruising speed: 675 km/h
Passengers: 110 or 122
Engines: Four turboprops

DATE _____

PLACE _____

INSIGNIA _____

LOCKHEED L 100 HERCULES

The Hercules is best known as a military plane, but civil versions have also been built. These carry freight. Services began in 1970 from the USA and Canada to the UK.

Wing span: 40·41 m
Length: 34·37 m
Cruising speed: 581 km/h
Freight: 23,505 kg
Engines: Four turboprops

DATE _____

PLACE _____

INSIGNIA _____

PILATUS BRITTEN-NORMAN ISLANDER

The Islander carries people from outlying areas to join major airline routes. It also provides services to out-of-the-way communities. Deliveries began in 1967. More than 1000 have been built.

Wing span: 14·94 m
Length: 10·86 m
Cruising speed: 257 km/h
Passengers: 9
Engines: Two piston engines

DATE _____

PLACE _____

INSIGNIA _____

PILATUS BRITTEN-NORMAN TRISLANDER

The Trislander is a larger version of the Islander. It has a longer fuselage, a high-mounted tailplane and a third engine in the fin.
Wing span: 16·15 m
Length: 15·01 m
Cruising speed: 267 km/h
Passengers: 18
Engines: Three piston engines

DATE _____

PLACE _____

INSIGNIA _____

SAAB-FAIRCHILD 340

This airliner went into service in 1984. It has been developed by a Swedish and an American company together. Crossair of Switzerland flies 340s to the UK.
Wing span: 21·44 m
Length: 19·71 m
Cruising speed: 508 km/h
Passengers: Up to 34
Engines: Two turboprops

DATE _____

PLACE _____

INSIGNIA _____

SHORTS BELFAST

The Belfast is a heavy long-range cargo freighter. It was built for the RAF, but offered for sale when retired in 1976. Today HeavyLift Cargo Airlines flies three. They are based at London's Stansted Airport.
Wing span: 48·41 m
Length: 41·58 m

Cruising speed: 510 km/h
Freight: 34,020 kg
Engines: Four turboprops

DATE _____

PLACE _____

INSIGNIA _____

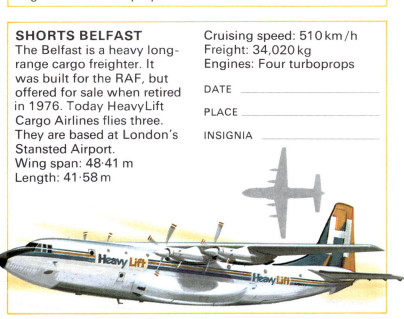

SHORTS 330

The Shorts 330 was designed for regional and commuter services. It was first used in Canada in 1976. More than 100 have been ordered. One UK operator is Loganair in Scotland.
Wing span: 22·76 m
Length: 17·69 m

Cruising speed: 352 km/h
Passengers: 30
Engines: Two turboprops

DATE _____

PLACE _____

INSIGNIA _____

SHORTS 360

The 360 is a lengthened development of the Shorts 330. It has the same type of square-section fuselage but uses a single tail fin and rudder. It first flew in 1981.
Wing span: 22·81 m
Length: 21·59 m
Cruising speed: 393 km/h

Passengers: 36
Engines: Two turboprops

DATE _____

PLACE _____

INSIGNIA _____

VICKERS MERCHANTMAN

The Vanguard passenger airliner was designed as a bigger version of the Viscount. The Merchantman first flew in 1969. It is a freighter made by conversion of the Vanguard.
Wing span: 36·15 m
Length: 37·45 m
Cruising speed: 684 km/h
Freight: Up to 18,500 kg
Engines: Four turboprops

DATE _____

PLACE _____

INSIGNIA _____

VICKERS VISCOUNT

More Viscounts are flown by British airlines than Merchantmen. This may seem surprising, as the Viscount is much older. In 1950 the Viscount became the first airliner with turboprop engines to carry paying passengers.
Wing span: 28·56 m
Length: 26·11 m
Cruising speed: 566 km/h
Passengers: 59 to 75
Engines: Four turboprops

DATE _____

PLACE _____

INSIGNIA _____

Helicopters

Helicopters are used in many ways. They carry passengers to or between airports, VIPs to business meetings, and workers to oil rigs at sea. Others spray crops to prevent blight, carry the sick to hospital and rescue people in danger.

Helicopters can do things aeroplanes cannot because they are able to hover in the air and take-off and land without a runway. An aeroplane uses its engines to gather enough speed to allow the wings to lift it into the air. A helicopter combines wings and a propeller in its rotor. The rotor has several thin blades which turn very quickly. This lifts the helicopter. By tilting the rotor slightly forward the helicopter goes forward. It can also fly sideways and backwards.

AÉROSPATIALE AS 350 ÉCUREUIL

This is a small French helicopter. The name Écureuil means Squirrel. It has a turboshaft engine. This is similar to a turboprop but turns a rotor not a propeller. A twin-engined version is the AS 355 Écureuil 2.

Rotor: 10·69 m
Length: 10·91 m
Cruising speed: 232 km/h
Seats: 6
Engine: One turboshaft

DATE _____

PLACE _____

INSIGNIA _____

AÉROSPATIALE SA 330 PUMA and AS 332 SUPER PUMA

The Puma is a medium-sized transport helicopter which first flew in 1965. The improved Super Puma flew in 1978. Bristow Helicopters uses these from Aberdeen, Yarmouth and the Shetland Islands.

Super Puma
Rotor: 15·60 m
Length: 15·52 m
Cruising speed: 280 km/h
Seats: 24
Engines: Two turboshafts

DATE _____

PLACE _____

INSIGNIA _____

BELL MODEL 47

The Bell 47 is one of the most important helicopters ever built. It was the first mass-produced civil helicopter. Model 47s were built from 1947 until 1976, mostly in America but finally in Italy. Look for the round 'bubble' canopy.

Rotor: 11·32 m
Length: 9·63 m
Seats: 3
Cruising speed: 135 km/h
Engine: One piston engine

DATE _____

PLACE _____

INSIGNIA _____

BELL MODEL 206 JETRANGER

The JetRanger is very popular. Many are owned privately in the UK or by business firms and air taxi operators. It has been in production since 1966. The newest version is the Model 206B JetRanger III.
Rotor: 10·16 m
Length: 9·50 m

Cruising speed: 216 km/h
Seats: 5
Engine: One turboshaft

DATE _____

PLACE _____

INSIGNIA _____

BELL MODEL 206L LONGRANGER

The LongRanger is a bigger version of the JetRanger. It has a longer fuselage and larger rotor. Hundreds of LongRangers have been built since 1975 and some fly in the UK.
Rotor: 11·28 m
Length: 10·13 m

Crusing speed: 203 km/h
Seats: 7
Engine: One turboshaft

DATE _____

PLACE _____

INSIGNIA _____

BOEING MODEL 234 COMMERCIAL CHINOOK

The largest helicopter operated in the UK. British Airways Helicopters ordered the very first examples for support operations to North Sea oil rigs. These went into service in 1981.
Rotors: 18·29 m each
Length: 15·87 m

Cruising speed: 269 km/h
Seats: 46
Engines: Two turboshafts

DATE _____

PLACE _____

INSIGNIA _____

ENSTROM MODEL F-28 and 280

The F-28 first flew in 1962. The improved Model 280 looks similar but has a downward pointing tailfin. It first flew in 1973.
F-28C-2
Rotor: 9·75 m
Length: 8·94 m
Cruising speed: 172 km/h

Seats: 3
Engine: One piston engine

DATE _____

PLACE _____

INSIGNIA _____

MBB BO 105

The BO 105 is a small but fast light helicopter. It comes from West Germany. Military and civil versions have been built since 1967. The pilot and co-pilot or passenger sit in the front. The rear bench seat can be taken out so that goods or stretchers can be carried in the roomy cabin.

DATE _____

PLACE _____

INSIGNIA _____

Rotor: 9·84 m
Length: 8·56 m
Cruising speed:
242 km/h
Seats: 5
Engines: Two turboshafts

SIKORSKY S-61

The American S-61 is a big and important helicopter. The S-61N version first flew in 1962. This can take off and land on water or dry land. Only 123 S-61Ns were built. British Airways, Bristow Helicopters and British Caledonian all use S-61Ns.

Rotor: 18·90 m
Length: 22·20 m (incl rotors)
Cruising speed: 222 km/h
Seats: 29 to 31
Engines: Two turboshafts

DATE _____

PLACE _____

INSIGNIA _____

SIKORSKY S-76

This helicopter first flew in 1977. It is very streamlined and fast. Many are regularly flown in the UK. It can be used for carrying passengers or goods, or for rescue and other roles. Like the smaller but similar Bell 222, its wheels can fold away after take-off.

Rotor: 13·41 m
Length: 16·00 m (incl rotors)
Cruising speed: 286 km/h
Seats: Up to 14
Engines: Two turboshafts

DATE _____

PLACE _____

INSIGNIA _____

WESTLAND 30

G·BIWY
British airways

A larger development of the military Lynx helicopter. It first flew in 1979. British Airways Helicopters was the first British user.

Rotor: 13·31 m
Length: 15·90 m
(including rotors)

Cruising speed: 222 km/h
Seats: Up to 21
Engines: Two turboshafts

DATE _____

PLACE _____

INSIGNIA _____

Business and Light Aircraft

There are many different types of business and light aircraft flying in the UK. The few described here have been chosen for their variety and shape. How many other types can you spot at airports, airfields and flying schools?

The term business aircraft means aircraft that are used to carry businessmen and executives. They can include small jet aircraft or piston-engined light planes. They often carry fewer people than similar aircraft used for normal passenger-carrying. This is because they may be very luxurious inside.

The term light aircraft means an aircraft which weighs less than 5670 kg at take-off. Many light planes are owned by their pilots and are flown for fun.

BAe HS 125
The 125 is a popular business transport aircraft. It has two small turbofan engines mounted on the rear fuselage. The first 125 flew in 1962. Many hundreds have been sold.
Wing span: 14·33 m
Length: 15·46 m
Cruising speed: 808 km/h

Passengers: Up to 14
Engines: Two turbofans

DATE _____

PLACE _____

INSIGNIA _____

BEECHCRAFT QUEEN AIR and KING AIR

The Queen Air business aircraft first flew in 1958. The King Air is similar. Look for the King Air's round (not square) side windows. It first flew in 1964.

King Air C90
Wing span: 15·32 m
Length: 10·82 m
Cruising speed: 412 km/h
Passengers: 4–8
Engines: Two turboprops

DATE _____

PLACE _____

INSIGNIA _____

CESSNA MODEL 152

The Model 152 first became available in 1977. It replaced the Model 150. More than 7000 have been built. It is a small cabin lightplane with a high-mounted wing.
Wing span: 9·97 m
Length: 7·34 m

Cruising speed: 196 km/h
Passengers: Pilot and passenger
Engine: One piston engine

DATE _____

PLACE _____

INSIGNIA _____

DASSAULT-BREGUET MYSTÈRE-FALCON 20

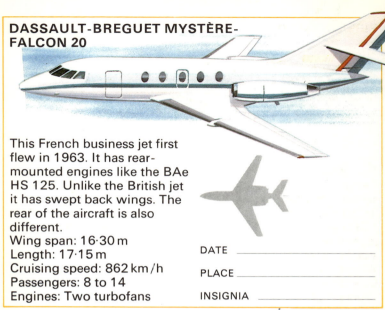

This French business jet first flew in 1963. It has rear-mounted engines like the BAe HS 125. Unlike the British jet it has swept back wings. The rear of the aircraft is also different.
Wing span: 16·30 m
Length: 17·15 m
Cruising speed: 862 km/h
Passengers: 8 to 14
Engines: Two turbofans

DATE _____

PLACE _____

INSIGNIA _____

PIPER NAVAJO and CHIEFTAIN

The Navajo is a business light transport aircraft. It can also be used as a commuter airliner. It first flew in 1964. The Chieftain is similar but has a longer fuselage and bigger engines. It first flew in 1972.

Navajo
Wing span: 12·40 m
Length: 9·94 m
Cruising speed: 407 km/h
Passengers: 5 to 7
Engines: Two piston engines

DATE _____

PLACE _____

INSIGNIA _____

PIPER TOMAHAWK

The Tomahawk is a training aircraft for flying schools. It became available in 1978. Within a year 1000 had been delivered. Instructor and pupil sit side by side in a roomy cabin.
Wing span: 10·36 m
Length: 7·04 m
Cruising speed: 200 km/h

Passengers: Pilot and pupil
Engine: One piston engine

DATE _____

PLACE _____

INSIGNIA _____

ROBIN DR 400 SERIES

The French DR 400 series covers several similar light planes. The prototype first flew in 1972. The DR 400/120 Dauphin, DR 400/160 Major, DR 400/180 Régent and glider-towing DR 400/ 180R Remorqueur are still being built.
Cruising speed: 245 km/h (Major)
Passengers: 1 to 3
Engine: One piston engine

DATE _____

PLACE _____

INSIGNIA _____

47

Index